CALIFORNIA

Explore the United States · Explore the United States · Explore the United States

Sarah Tieck

Big Buddy BOOKS
Explore the United States

VISIT US AT
www.abdopublishing.com

Published by ABDO Publishing Company, PO Box 398166, Minneapolis, MN 55439.

Printed in the United States of America, North Mankato, Minnesota.
022012
092012

 PRINTED ON RECYCLED PAPER

Coordinating Series Editor: Rochelle Baltzer
Contributing Editors: BreAnn Rumsch, Marcia Zappa
Graphic Design: Adam Craven
Cover Photograph: *Shutterstock*: somchaij.
Interior Photographs/Illustrations: *AP Photo*: AP Photo (p. 25), Chris Pizzello (p. 23), PAUL SAKUMA/AP/dapd
       (p. 23), David Stluka (p. 21); *Getty Images*: Kean Collection/Archive Photos/Getty Images (p. 13), David McNew
       (p. 25); *iStockphoto*: iStockphoto.com/JasonDoiy (p. 19), iStockphoto.com/holgs (p. 27), iStockphoto.com/
       jimkruger (p. 27), iStockphoto.com/Pgiam (p. 29), iStockphoto.com/SDbT (p. 21); *Shutterstock*: Juan Camilo
       Bernal (p. 26), Johann Helgason (p. 19), Mariusz S. Jurgielewicz (pp. 5, 30), Jeffrey T. Kreulen (p. 17), Phillip
       Lange (p. 30), Chee-Onn Leong (p. 27), Steve Minkler (p. 11), Nagel Photography (p. 11), Glenn Price (p. 30),
       urosr (p. 30), Andy Z. (p. 9).

All population figures taken from the 2010 US census.

Library of Congress Cataloging-in-Publication Data

Tieck, Sarah, 1976-
  California / Sarah Tieck.
     p. cm. -- (Explore the United States)
  ISBN 978-1-61783-343-4
  1. California--Juvenile literature. I. Title.
  F861.3.T54 2013
  979.4--dc23
                        2012000755

Contents

ONE NATION

The United States is a **diverse** country. It has farmland, cities, coasts, and mountains. Its people come from many different backgrounds. And, its history covers more than 200 years.

Today the country includes 50 states. California is one of these states. Let's learn more about California and its story!

Did You Know?

California became a state on September 9, 1850. It was the thirty-first state to join the nation.

California borders the Pacific Ocean.

CALIFORNIA UP CLOSE

Did You Know?

Washington DC is the US capital city. Puerto Rico is a US commonwealth. This means it is governed by its own people.

The United States has four main **regions**. California is in the West.

California borders three states. Oregon is north. Nevada and Arizona are east. The country of Mexico is south. And, the Pacific Ocean is west.

California is the third-largest state. It has a total area of 158,608 square miles (410,793 sq km). The state has the highest population in the country. More than 37 million people live there.

REGIONS OF THE UNITED STATES

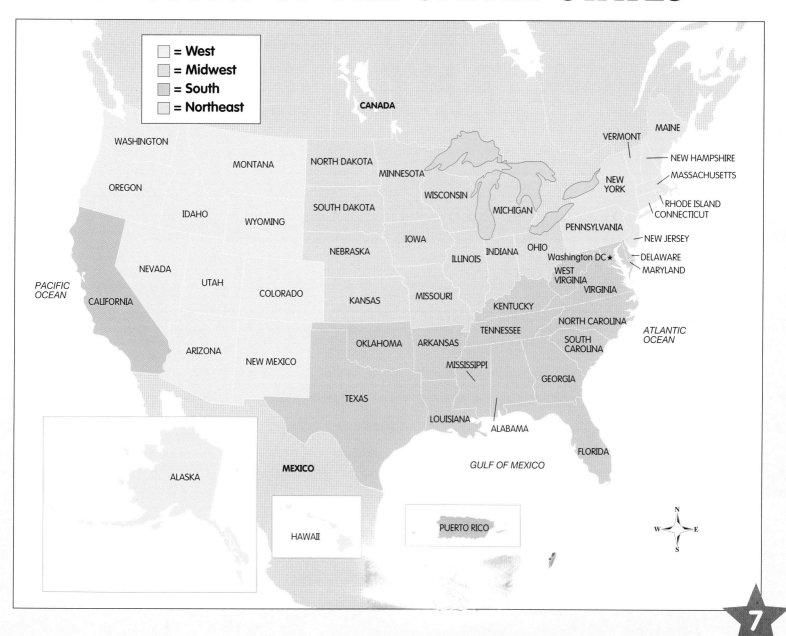

= West
= Midwest
= South
= Northeast

CANADA

WASHINGTON
MONTANA
NORTH DAKOTA
MINNESOTA
VERMONT
MAINE
NEW HAMPSHIRE
MASSACHUSETTS
OREGON
IDAHO
WYOMING
SOUTH DAKOTA
WISCONSIN
MICHIGAN
NEW YORK
RHODE ISLAND
CONNECTICUT
PENNSYLVANIA
NEW JERSEY
IOWA
NEBRASKA
ILLINOIS
INDIANA
OHIO
Washington DC ★
DELAWARE
MARYLAND
NEVADA
UTAH
COLORADO
WEST VIRGINIA
VIRGINIA
PACIFIC OCEAN
CALIFORNIA
KANSAS
MISSOURI
KENTUCKY
NORTH CAROLINA
ATLANTIC OCEAN
TENNESSEE
SOUTH CAROLINA
ARIZONA
NEW MEXICO
OKLAHOMA
ARKANSAS
MISSISSIPPI
GEORGIA
TEXAS
LOUISIANA
ALABAMA
FLORIDA
GULF OF MEXICO
ALASKA
MEXICO
HAWAII
PUERTO RICO

N
W E
S

7

IMPORTANT CITIES

Sacramento is the **capital** of California. It is in the northern part of the state. This area is known as Gold Country. That's because gold was found there in 1848.

Los Angeles is the largest city in the state. It is in southern California near the Pacific Ocean. Nearly 4 million people live there. That makes it the second-largest city in the United States!

Did You Know?

After gold was found near Sacramento, thousands of people moved there. This was called the gold rush.

CALIFORNIA

Sacramento
San Francisco
Los Angeles
San Diego

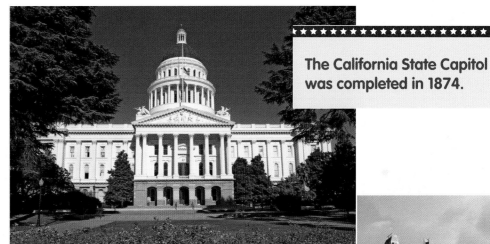

The California State Capitol was completed in 1874.

Los Angeles is home to many writers, actors, and musicians. It is a place where television shows and films are made.

Sacramento is located where the Sacramento and American Rivers meet.

9

San Diego is California's second-largest city. Its population is 1,307,402. It was founded in 1769. It is the state's oldest city. Some people call this city the birthplace of California.

San Francisco is another important city in the state. It is home to the Golden Gate Bridge. This bridge is 8,981 feet (2,737 m) long. It is one of the world's longest **suspension bridges**.

Millions of people cross the Golden Gate Bridge every year.

San Diego is known for its deepwater harbor.

CALIFORNIA IN HISTORY

California's history includes explorers, war, and **frontier** life. Beginning in 1769, Spanish explorers settled land in present-day California. Native Americans had lived there for thousands of years.

From 1846 to 1848, the United States and Mexico fought over land. This was called the Mexican-American War. After the war, California became part of the United States. Around this time, gold was found there. Many people moved to the new frontier and settled the land.

The gold rush brought people to California from all over the world. They used pans, shovels, and axes to search for gold.

13

Timeline

1769

Spanish explorers settled land in California.

1821

Mexico became independent from Spain. California became part of Mexico.

1850

California became a state on September 9.

1869

The Central Pacific Railroad line, which started in Sacramento, was completed. The railroad was the first to cross the United States.

1700s

1800s

The Mexican-American War began. When the war ended in 1848, California became part of the United States.

The gold rush began. For the next few years, many people came to California to find gold.

1846

1848

14

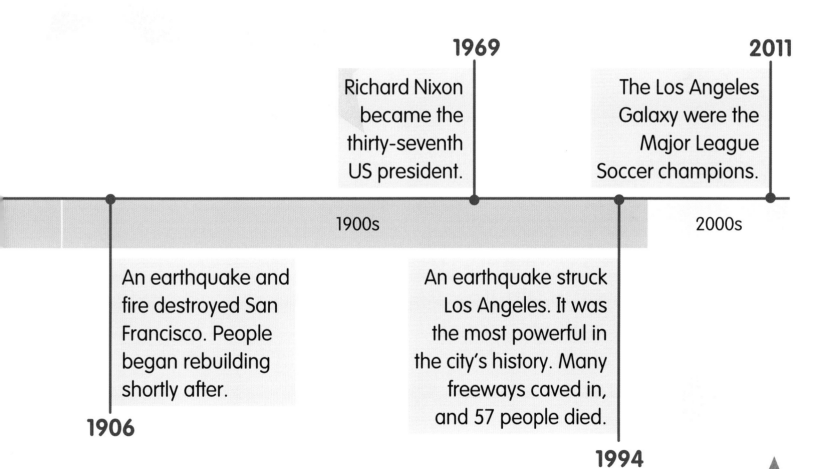

1969

Richard Nixon became the thirty-seventh US president.

2011

The Los Angeles Galaxy were the Major League Soccer champions.

1900s

2000s

An earthquake and fire destroyed San Francisco. People began rebuilding shortly after.

An earthquake struck Los Angeles. It was the most powerful in the city's history. Many freeways caved in, and 57 people died.

1906

1994

ACROSS THE LAND

California has forests, deserts, mountains, and beaches. Death Valley is in southeastern California. It has the lowest point on Earth's western half. Mount Whitney is near the middle of the state. It is the highest point in the **continental** United States.

Many types of animals make their homes in California. Some of these include black bears, quails, and rattlesnakes.

Death Valley is known for extreme temperatures. In 1913, the air was 134°F (57°C) in the shade. This is the hottest such temperature ever recorded in North America!

EARNING A LIVING

Farming and banking are important businesses in California. The state is also known for making movies and television shows.

Many **technology** companies are in California. These produce computers and other **electronics**. They provide jobs for people in California.

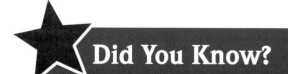

Did You Know?

California grows more than half the country's supply of fruits and vegetables! Grapes, oranges, tomatoes, and lettuce are major crops in the state.

Since the 1970s, California has been known for making electronics, such as computer chips.

Yahoo!, Google, and Apple are some of the large technology companies based in California.

19

Sports Page

California is home to many sports teams. These include baseball, basketball, football, soccer, and hockey teams. California also hosts important golf and tennis events. And, car and motorcycle races are held in the state.

College sports are popular in California. Pasadena hosts the Rose Bowl every January. Two top college football teams play in the Rose Bowl. The game has been played at the Rose Bowl stadium since 1922.

Did You Know?

California hosted the Olympic Games in 1932, 1960, and 1984.

The 2012 game set a record for the highest-scoring Rose Bowl. The University of Oregon beat the University of Wisconsin 45–38.

Pebble Beach is a famous golf course in California. The US Open is sometimes played there.

HOMETOWN HEROES

Many famous people are from California. Steve Jobs was born in San Francisco in 1955. He was famous for helping to start Apple Inc. Apple makes computers, iPods, and other **electronics**.

Filmmaker George Lucas was born in Modesto in 1944. He created the Star Wars and Indiana Jones movies. His work has won many awards.

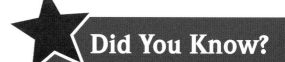

Did You Know?

In 1986, Jobs bought Pixar Animation Studios, which was started by Lucas. Pixar became famous for making movies such as *Toy Story*.

Jobs died in 2011. His company and ideas changed the way people use computers.

Lucas has made some of the most popular films in history.

23

Richard M. Nixon is another famous Californian. Nixon was born in Yorba Linda in 1913. He was the US president from 1969 to 1974.

Nixon was known for working with other countries. He helped end the **Vietnam War**. And, he was the first active president to visit China. In 1974, Nixon became the first person to quit his job as US president.

The Nixon Presidential Library and Museum is in Yorba Linda. It has items from Nixon's life and time as president. The house he grew up in is there, too!

Nixon was the thirty-seventh US president.

Tour Book

Do you want to go to California? If you visit the state, here are some places to go and things to do!

★ Cheer

Californians are proud of their sports teams. Watch the Los Angeles Lakers play basketball at Staples Center!

★ See

Hollywood is a part of Los Angeles where many movies have been made. You might see a movie star there! Look for the Hollywood sign in the hills above the city.

26

★ Discover

Go for a hike in Yosemite National Park. You will see forests, streams, mountains, and valleys.

★ Visit

The San Diego Zoo is one of the world's largest zoos. It is home to about 4,000 animals, including giant pandas.

★ Ride

San Francisco is known for having hilly streets. People can ride cable cars up and down some of these streets.

A Great State

The story of California is important to the United States. The people and places that make up this state offer something special to the country. Together with all the states, California helps make the United States great.

Did You Know?

The world's largest tree is one of California's giant sequoias. It is about 275 feet (84 m) tall. Its base is more than 100 feet (30 m) around!

★★★★★★★★★★★★★★★★★★★★★★★★★★★★★★★★★★★★★★

California is home to many natural wonders, such as giant sequoia (sih-KWOI-uh) redwood trees.

Fast Facts

Date of Statehood:
September 9, 1850

State Capital:
Sacramento

Postal Abbreviation:
CA

Population (rank):
37,253,956
(most populated state)

Flag:

Tree: California Redwood

Total Area (rank):
158,608 square miles
(3rd largest state)

Motto:
"Eureka"
(I Have Found It)

Flower: California Poppy

Bird: California Valley Quail

Nickname:
Golden State

30

Important Words

capital a city where government leaders meet.
continental being part of the United States made up of the lower 48 states.
diverse made up of things that are different from each other.
electronics products that work by controlling the flow of electricity. These often do useful things.
frontier the edge of settled land, where unsettled land begins.
region a large part of a country that is different from other parts.
suspension bridge a bridge that has its roadway hanging from cables.
technology (tehk-NAH-luh-jee) the use of science for practical purposes.
Vietnam War a war that took place between South Vietnam and North Vietnam from 1957 to 1975. The United States was involved in this war for many years.

Web Sites

To learn more about California, visit ABDO Publishing Company online. Web sites about California are featured on our Book Links page. These links are routinely monitored and updated to provide the most current information available.

www.abdopublishing.com

31

Index